CATHOLIC ANSWERS TO CONTEMPORARY QUESTIONS

Daniel L. Lowery, C.SS.R.

LIGUORI
PUBLICATIONS

One Liguori Drive
Liguori, Missouri 63057-9999
(314) 464-2500

Imprimi Potest:
James Shea, C.SS.R.
Provincial, St. Louis Province
The Redemptorists

Imprimatur:
Monsignor Maurice F. Byrne
Vice Chancellor, Archdiocese of St. Louis

ISBN 0-89243-410-4
Library of Congress Catalog Card Number: 91-62106

Copyright © 1991, Liguori Publications
Printed in U.S.A.

Cover design by Pam Hummelsheim

CONTENTS

Introduction 5

Part I. Faith Questions

1. What Is Meant by Original Sin? 7
2. Why Does the Church Allow Infant Baptism? 10
3. Why Doesn't the Church Require Circumcision? 13
4. Just What Is a Mortal Sin? 15
5. How Can I Get More Out of the Mass? 17
6. How Should Sunday Be Kept Holy? 19
7. Are Distractions in Prayer Normal? 22
8. Are Laypeople Called to Holiness? 24
9. Should I Be More Involved in the Church? 26
10. What Is a Retreat? 28
11. How Should a Person Prepare for Death? 30
12. What Must I Believe About Purgatory? 33
13. Does Hell Exist? 35
14. What Does the Church Teach About Heaven? 38

Part II. Moral Questions

15. Do People Who Commit Suicide Go to Hell? 41
16. Is Capital Punishment Right or Wrong? 43
17. Why Is the Catholic Church So Opposed
    to Abortion? 46
18. What Is the Church's Position
    on Artificial Fertilization? 49

19. Is There a Difference Between Active and
    Passive Euthanasia? 53
20. What Is a Living Will? 55
21. What Is a "Christian Response" to AIDS? 58
22. How Can I Deal With My Anger? 61
23. What Can I Do About Jealousy? 64
24. How Much Should I Give to the Poor? 66
25. Is Racism a Sin? 68
26. Is There a Handy Moral Code for Employees? 70
27. Is There a Handy Moral Code for Employers? 73
28. What Does the Church Say About
    Interfaith Marriages? 76

INTRODUCTION

In 1984 Liguori Publications published a booklet of mine: *Catholic Beliefs, Laws, Practices: 26 Questions and Answers.* I was pleased with the wide distribution of this publication, and even more pleased with some of the people who wrote to me in response to it. Some of these people took issue with my answers, but more asked new questions. I have come to believe that almost every Catholic has a good question or two up his or her sleeve!

Since 1984 I have been involved part time in the teaching of moral theology and in writing for Catholic publications. In both of these situations, I have received new questions about Catholic faith and morals. This book addresses some of these questions. These really are "questions people ask."

For the sake of convenience, I have divided the material into two main parts. Part I deals with "Faith Questions." Many of the entries in this section come from Catholics or from people who are thinking about joining the Catholic community. For the most part, they are concerned with particular beliefs or practices of the Catholic Church. Others, however, might be of interest to a wider audience: questions such as "Are Laypeople Called to Holiness?" and "How Should a Person Prepare for Death?"

Part II addresses "Moral Questions." Many of these entries are of concern not only to Catholics but to many other persons as well. It is also true, however, that the Catholic Church has directly addressed itself to many of these questions and has provided some definite answers and guidelines.

I have tried to treat all the questions in this book with respect. In answering them, I have tried to state clearly official Catholic teaching when that is available; in other cases, I have tried to offer what seems to me a balanced response in the tradition of Catholic theology.

Some of these questions and answers have appeared in shorter form in the Sunday bulletins of Liguori Publications. I wish to thank the editor for permission to use them here.

It is often said that the Irish answer a question with another question. If, as you read this book, new questions occur to you, let me hear from you. There's always room for another book!

I am grateful to the men and women who have supplied the questions that are answered here. I hope that my answers will be of help to them as well as to others who may chance to read them. To all, blessings and peace.

Daniel L. Lowery, C.SS.R.

PART I

FAITH QUESTIONS

1. What Is Meant by Original Sin?

Dear Father,
   A visiting priest comes to our parish every weekend. His homilies are wonderful. But he often uses phrases like "That's because of original sin" or "We shouldn't forget about original sin." I'm not sure what he means. What is meant by original sin?

Melanie

Dear Melanie,

Your question is certainly important, and also difficult to answer in a short space. In the long course of Christian history, there have been whole volumes written on the meaning of original sin. Here I can give only a basic answer to your question.

The Second Vatican Council states: "Although set by God in a state of rectitude, man, enticed by the evil one, abused his freedom at the very start of history. He lifted himself up against

God, and sought to attain his goal apart from him" (*Pastoral Constitution on the Church in the Modern World,* #13). This is a concise description of original sin, the sin that occurred at the origin of the human race.

The Book of Genesis tells the story of that original sin in striking detail. The first two chapters of Genesis tell how God created all things, including man and woman, and saw that they were "very good." In chapter 3, however, Adam rejects God and separates himself from him. Adam tries to hide from God, blames Eve for his sin, and experiences the pangs of guilt.

From the original sin of Adam, a host of evils came into the world. Chapters 4 through 11 of Genesis describe in narrative form how the first sin brought a "mushroom cloud" of evil into the world. Cain murders his brother Abel in cold blood. Sin is so rampant that God sends a great Flood (from which only Noah and his family are preserved). That Flood highlights the chaos and destruction brought by sin into the beauty of creation.

Yet even this does not open the eyes of the people. Chapter 11 of Genesis tells the story of human beings still defying God and wanting to be his equal by building a tower that would reach to the heavens. The Tower of Babel, as it is called, speaks eloquently about the effects of sin: Human beings not only reject God but also reject and despise one another. There is now division and hatred among nations.

"According to Genesis, a world of beauty was deformed by sin. The ongoing result has been division, pain, bloodshed, loneliness, and death. This tragic narrative has a familiar ring to it. The reality it points to is a basic part of human experience. It is no surprise that this reality — the fact of original sin and its effects in us all — is a teaching of the Church" (*Handbook for Today's Catholic,* Liguori Publications, page 27).

It is the teaching of the Church, Melanie, that every mortal born into this world, except the Virgin Mary, is affected by original sin. This is not a personal sin committed by each individual (such as lying or stealing), but rather, in the words of Pope Paul VI, "It is human nature so fallen, stripped of the grace that clothes it, injured in its own natural powers and subjected to the dominion of death, that is transmitted to all men and women, and it is in this sense that every person is born in sin" (*Credo of the People of God*). Original sin means, therefore, that each "descendant of Adam" (that includes us) is created without sanctifying grace (new life in Christ) and is subject to concupiscence — the inclination to sin — as well as the punishment of death.

To put it another way, original sin refers to the wounded human condition that all people experience. This is described very well by Catholic historian Berard Marthaler, O.F.M., Conv.: "Looked at from the outside, original sin names the human condition — the broken covenant, the universal estrangement, the ambiguous predicament — that is the lot of every individual born into a world where sin reigns" (*The Creed,* Twenty-Third Publications, page 98).

Yet, at the same time, the Catholic Church, unlike some of the Protestant reformers, rejects the idea that human nature as such is corrupt. True, it is weak and inconstant, but it is not completely incapable of good acts or free choices. Above all, fallen human nature is capable of receiving sanctifying grace through the death and resurrection of Jesus Christ.

While you should not forget about original sin, as your visiting priest asserts, you must also not slip into the error of thinking that sin is somehow more powerful than God's grace. Gabriel Daly makes this point very clearly: "Sound theology must show that the scope and power of sin are always abundantly exceeded by the scope and power of grace and the salvific will of God" (*New Dictionary of Theology,* Michael Glazier, Inc., page 731).

Saint Paul underlines this same theme when he writes: "For if by that one person's [Adam's] transgression the many died, how much more did the grace of God and the gracious gift of the one person Jesus Christ overflow for the many" (Romans 5:15). This grace of God, this new life in Christ, is passed on especially through the sacrament of Baptism, Melanie, and so the darkness of original sin is overcome by the bright victory of Christ over all sin and death. Praise the Lord!

2. Why Does the Church Allow Infant Baptism?

Dear Father,

I am Catholic; one of my best friends is Baptist. She feels strongly that the Catholic Church is wrong in allowing infant Baptism. She says that children should be old enough to understand what is going on. Why does the Church allow infant Baptism?

Jean

Dear Jean,

To answer your question, I would simply like to explain what the Catholic Church teaches about this matter. Perhaps you can share this with your friend. Though it may not convince her, at least it will give her a clearer understanding of the Catholic position.

In 1980 the Vatican's Congregation of the Faith issued an *Instruction on Infant Baptism* which states: "From the earliest times, the church, to which the preaching of the gospel and baptizing was entrusted, has baptized infants as well as adults." The practice of baptizing infants is "a rule of immemorial tradition."

Historically, this certainly seems to be true. As early as the second century there is strong evidence that this was the practice of the Christian community. Among many others, Saint Iranaeus (about A.D. 180) considers it a matter of course that "infants and small children," as well as adults, should be baptized. A few early theologians did voice opposition to infant Baptism, but their very opposition indicated that the practice was common in the Church.

Infant Baptism did not become controversial until the time of the Reformation. At that time not only Catholics but also Lutherans and Calvinists strongly defended the traditional practice. "On the other side," explains Berard Marthaler, "were the 'anabaptists,'...because of their practice of rebaptizing persons who had been baptized as infants. The anabaptists... insisted on a personal confession of faith as a requisite for true baptism" (*The Creed,* Twenty-Third Publications, page 343). The present-day Baptists, as well as some other churches, also demand this personal profession of faith and therefore oppose infant Baptism, as your friend has already told you.

Shortly before his death, Pope Paul VI restated the centuries-old teaching of the Church in this way: "Baptism should be conferred even on infants who are unable to commit any sin personally, in order that, having been born without supernatural grace, they might be born again of water and the Holy Spirit to divine life in Christ Jesus" *(Instruction,* #8).

This teaching obviously echoes the teaching of Jesus himself: "No one can enter the kingdom of God without being born of water and Spirit" (John 3:5). The Church considers this an invitation of universal and limitless love, an invitation that applies to children as well as adults. In fact, according to the above-mentioned *Instruction,* "The Church...knows no other way apart from baptism for ensuring children's entry into eternal happiness" (#13).

Your friend emphasizes, Jean, that those to be baptized should be old enough to understand what is going on. This is an understandable concern. But must the special gift of God's grace and love be limited to adults only? After all, as the *Instruction* says, "In reality the child is a person long before [he or she] can show [this] by acts of consciousness and freedom. As a person, the child is already capable of becoming, through the sacrament of baptism, a child of God and a coheir with Christ" (#20).

Baptism is always a faith celebration. It is important to understand that the infant is baptized "into the faith of the Church." The child enters a faith community that already exists — one that is an ongoing and dynamic reality. It does not have to be re-created at each new Baptism. An infant becomes a citizen of the United States by being born of American citizens. The child thus enters into a society that already exists. So, too, through Baptism the infant enters the community of faith and becomes a true member of that community.

Furthermore, "the faith is proclaimed for them by their parents and godparents, who represent both the local Church and the whole society of saints and believers." This is not odd. Parents feed infants because they know they need food and that this kind of food is good for them. They do not wait until their children are old enough to freely choose food for themselves. As in many areas of life, parents also take responsibility for the faith life of their children; they profess faith in the name of each of their children.

But, Jean, infant Baptism does not imply that children never have to take responsibility for their Baptism. The parents promise to give their offspring an opportunity to be educated and formed in the faith of their Baptism. As the children grow in this Christian formation, however, they must at some point make their own decision about Baptism by either ratifying it or denying it. The fact that young adults, provided they have had basic Christian education, decide not to be practicing Catholics does not mean that the parents did something wrong in having the children baptized. It means only that the young adults are free to make their own choice about the implications of Baptism.

I hope, Jean, that these few lines give some answer to your question and perhaps some insight to your friend.

3. Why Doesn't the Church Require Circumcision?

Dear Father,
I know that the Jews practice circumcision as a sign of God's covenant with them. If this action was prescribed by God as a sign of the covenant, why don't Catholics have to continue the rite? Thank you for any information you can give me.

William

Dear William,

To avoid any misunderstandings, I would like to emphasize that in my answer to your letter, I am considering circumcision in a religious sense, not in a medical sense. Medically, circumcision seems to have become almost routine in the United States. Some people do not think this is a good idea. There is an ongoing debate about this topic. In answering your letter, I do not intend to say anything pro or con about this debate.

For the Hebrews, as you have pointed out, circumcision clearly had — and still has — a deep religious meaning. The Book of Genesis depicts the Lord saying to Abram: "Between you and me I will establish my covenant, and I will multiply you exceedingly....You are to become the father of a host of nations....I will maintain my covenant with you and your descendants after you throughout the ages as an everlasting pact" (17:2, 4, 7).

Then, after changing his name from Abram to Abraham (see Genesis 17:5), the Lord tells him: "This is my covenant with you and your descendants after you that you must keep: every male among you shall be circumcised. Circumcise the flesh of your foreskin, and that shall be the mark of the covenant between you and me. Throughout the ages, every male...shall be circumcised....Thus my covenant shall be in your flesh as an everlasting pact. If a male is uncircumcised...such a one shall be cut off from his people; he has broken my covenant" (Genesis 17:10-14).

Turning from the Hebrew to the Christian Scriptures: John the Baptizer was circumcised on the eighth day after his birth (see Luke 1:59) and so too was Jesus (see Luke 2:21). Saint Paul says that he was "circumcised on the eighth day" (Philippians 3:5). Jewish members of the early Christian community were often referred to as simply "the circumcised" (see Acts of Apostles 11:2). As I mentioned above, the religious significance of circumcision is still held in high esteem by the Jewish people.

In the primitive Christian community, however, a serious dispute arose about circumcision. The dispute settled around the question: Must gentile converts to Christianity be circumcised? Some of the Jewish Christians insisted on circumcision for the Gentile converts: "Unless you are circumcised according to the Mosaic practice, you cannot be saved" (Acts of the Apostles 15:1). Others insisted that circumcision, as a religious rite, was no longer necessary.

The Council of Jerusalem (the first of the ecumenical councils in the Church) took up this as well as other similar questions. After much debate, the Council, with Saint Peter as spokesman, made it clear there was no need to impose the Mosaic law on the gentile Christians. "We believe that we are saved through the grace of the Lord Jesus, in the same way as they" (Acts of the Apostles 15:11).

In his New Testament Letters, Paul frequently returns to the theme that circumcision as a religious rite is no longer necessary, that salvation comes from the redeeming death of Christ and not from the practice of the Mosaic law. "For in Christ Jesus, neither circumcision nor uncircumcision counts for anything, but only faith working through love" (Galatians 5:6; see also Galatians 6:15; Romans 3:30).

While respecting the beliefs of the Hebrew community, William, the Catholic Church professes that persons become adopted sons and daughters of God through Baptism, and it is their faith that binds them to salvation. From a religious standpoint, therefore, circumcision is no longer required.

4. Just What Is a Mortal Sin?

Dear Father,
I would like to see a treatment of mortal sin. Today it seems nobody knows what it is. I wish there could be an article that makes it clear, black and white.

Edgar

Dear Father,
We are taught that we may receive holy Communion provided we are free of mortal sin. Is there some kind of list that can be followed? What is it that makes a sin mortal?

Donna

Dear Edgar and Donna,

I am going to try to give a basic answer to your questions. My answer may not be as black and white as you would like, Edgar, and it may not include the kind of list you are looking for, Donna, but I hope it will provide the beginning of a response to your questions.

Concerning the fundamental idea of mortal sin (also called "serious" or "grave" sin in Church literature), we are fortunate to have an explanation from the supreme teacher of our Church, Pope John Paul II. In his far-ranging *Apostolic Exhor-*

tation on Reconciliation and Penance (1984), the Pope traced the Biblical teaching on sin together with the teaching of the great Fathers and Doctors of the Church which he summarized as follows:

> With the whole tradition of the Church, we call mortal sin the act by which a person freely and consciously rejects God, his law, the covenant of love that God offers, preferring to turn in on himself or to some created and finite reality, something contrary to the divine will. This can occur in a direct and formal way in the sins of idolatry, apostasy, and atheism; or in an equivalent way as in every act of disobedience to God's commandments in grave matter. Man perceives that this disobedience to God destroys the bond that unites him with his life principle: It is a mortal sin, that is, an act which gravely offends God and ends in turning against man himself with a dark and powerful force of destruction.

Further on, the Pope also emphasizes the Church's traditional teaching (found in all the old catechisms) that "mortal sin is sin whose object is grave matter and which is also committed with full knowledge and deliberate consent."

I'm sure you will agree with me, Edgar, that this teaching of the Pope on mortal sin is quite clear. It does demand a certain amount of thought and reflection, but all in all it is a clear statement of Catholic teaching.

That still leaves Donna's question about a list of mortal sins. While the Holy Father does not give a list as such, he does encourage Christians to examine their consciences in the light of the twofold commandment to love God above all and to love their neighbors as themselves and the Ten Commandments as given in the Old Testament and as confirmed and refined by Jesus himself (see Matthew 5:17-48). Pope John Paul II also urges Christians not to overlook sins against justice in personal relationships, sins against the rights of the human person, and sins against the common good of society.

The Holy Father explicitly calls people's attention to two texts from the Letter to the Romans, Donna, that should help them to spot sin in their own lives. This Letter speaks of those who "are filled with every form of wickedness, evil, greed, and malice; full of envy, murder, rivalry, treachery, and spite. They are gossips and scandalmongers and they hate God. They are insolent, haughty, boastful, ingenious in their wickedness, and rebellious toward their parents" (Romans 1:29-30). The same Letter insists that we "conduct ourselves properly as in the day, not in orgies and drunkenness, not in promiscuity and licentiousness, not in rivalry and jealousy" (Romans 13:13).

In short, Edgar and Donna, I think the above is a clear description of mortal sin as well as many concrete examples against which all people can measure their own conduct and honestly discover if they have been guilty of mortal sin.

5. How Can I Get More Out of the Mass?

Dear Father,

I hope you won't think I'm boasting, but I can honestly say that, except for times when I was ill, I have never missed Sunday Mass. Yet I sometimes feel like I'm in a rut. I often wonder how I could put more into and get more out of my attendance at Mass. Do you have any suggestions?

Al

Dear Al,

First, let me say that I truly admire your fidelity to the Mass. That fidelity, even if you sometimes feel in a rut, is wonderful evidence of your love for God. I am going to offer you a few suggestions for getting more out of the Mass. I hope they will be helpful to you and to others as well.

The most fundamental guideline the Church proposes is this: Catholics are called to "take part knowingly, actively, and fruitfully" in the Mass. At first glance, that guideline seems almost too simple to be helpful, yet it offers numerous possibilities.

Take part knowingly: The more people know about the Mass, the better they will participate in it. Most Catholics have some basic knowledge and information about the Mass. Yet for many that knowledge was acquired years ago and was perhaps better suited to childhood or adolescence than to adulthood. In almost every sphere of life, they understand that what they learned as children is not adequate for adulthood. So, too, with their religious knowledge.

For this reason I believe it is very important for adults to review and refresh their knowledge of the Mass. This can be done, for example, by reading a contemporary theology book on the Eucharist, by studying an up-to-date adult catechism, by attending some classes, or by watching and discussing with others a video that explains the Mass. Any method that broadens and deepens their knowledge of the Mass is bound to help them in their worship.

Take part actively: Surely one of the most important thrusts of Vatican II was its emphasis on "active participation" at Mass. Gathered as a community of God's people, Catholics come not as strangers or rugged individualists or passive spectators — as at a movie or play — but as faith-filled participants.

Experience shows that even devout Catholics can easily be sidetracked by outside distractions such as poor acoustics or crying babies or late-arriving adults. That is why it is very helpful to prepare for the Sunday liturgy before actually participating in it. Meditating on the prayers and Scripture readings beforehand can bring a new richness to the participants. Properly prepared, they will be able to join in the singing, praying, listening, and responding with an alert spirit.

Take part fruitfully: The fruits of the Mass should extend to the daily lives of those who participate in it. I suggest, Al, that you try to "take something home" from Mass. One way of doing this is to sum up in a phrase or sentence what you have experienced. This might be a phrase from one of the hymns. For example, the Mass at which I presided last week concluded with the hymn "Now Thank We All Our God." I tried to bring a spirit of gratitude out of church with me; I tried to be more aware that day of all the wonderful blessings God has given me. Or it might be a sentence from one of the Scripture readings or from the homily. Such a summary can also serve as a good focus for prayer during the coming week.

These suggestions — fuller knowledge of the Mass, better preparation, and creative use of its benefits — are certainly not dramatic, but I hope they are of some help to you, Al. Most of all, I want to repeat what I said at the beginning: I believe your fidelity to the Mass is wonderful evidence of your love for God, and I know this is very pleasing to him.

6. How Should Sunday Be Kept Holy?

Dear Father,

Would you please explain the Church's rules in regard to keeping the Sabbath holy? What type of work is permissible and what is not? For example, during the harvest season, can a farmer farm his fields on Sunday or harvest his crops? Can a teacher grade papers or write tests? Thank you for your time and attention.

Tom

Dear Tom,

Rather than begin with an answer to your specific questions, I would like to suggest some basic convictions of the Catholic community in regard to Sunday.

The third commandment, "Remember to keep holy the sabbath day" (Exodus 20:8), was given by God to the people of Israel at a period of time in their history when they lived in a religiously hostile environment. The Sabbath commemorated how God rested on the seventh day, after he had completed the six days of creation. In memory of this, the seventh day should always be kept holy. The full text of this commandment spells out how the Sabbath was to be kept holy: "No work may be done then either by you, or your son or daughter, or your male or female slave, or your beast, or by the alien who lives with you" (Exodus 20:10). But abstinence from work was not an end in itself. The day was a "sabbath for the Lord." Abstinence from work was a way of worshiping God.

The Christian community very early chose Sunday, not the Sabbath (Saturday), as their special day of the week. Sunday was chosen in memory of that key day in history when Jesus Christ rose from the dead "on the first day of the week" (John 20:1). That day was considered the first day of the "new creation" in which Christians share.

It is essential to understand, Tom, that Sunday observance is specifically Christian. It is different from the Jewish Sabbath. In their excellent booklet, *The Ten Commandments and Today's Christian* (Liguori Publications), Finbarr Connolly and Peter Burns explain this well:

Sunday is not primarily a day of rest from work. Historically, the laws about servile work on Sunday probably owe more to the remnants of the Jewish sabbath than to the celebration of the Lord's Day. In a word, Sunday is the Lord's Day, when we celebrate the Resurrection of Christ!

We do indeed keep this day "holy." The Hebrew word *holy* means "different." For us, Sunday is a day in the week which is different in the sense that it belongs to God. It is different in that it should be a day of rest. A day of rest, however, need not mean that one is tied down to a day of total inactivity.

The revised Code of Canon Law clearly summarizes Catholic teaching about the Lord's Day: "Sunday is the day on which the paschal mystery is celebrated in light of the apostolic tradition and is to be observed as the foremost holy day of obligation....On Sundays and other holy days of obligation the faithful are bound to participate in the Mass; they are also to abstain from those labors and business concerns which impede the worship to be rendered to God, the joy which is proper to the Lord's Day, or the proper relaxation of mind and body" (Canons 1246, #1; 1247).

In light of these reflections, Tom, you can see that Catholics are challenged to make conscientious decisions about what work is permissible on Sunday and what is not. Obviously, some people are obliged from the very nature of their jobs to work on Sunday. Many other people seldom, if ever, are required to work on Sunday. When this is the case, every person has to ask himself or herself: Is Sunday a holy, different day for me? Or is it in effect "business as usual"?

Returning to the specific questions of your letter, I would ask: Do the farmer and the teacher you refer to celebrate the Eucharist with the Christian community? Have they without necessity made Sunday just another day of work or business, or do they still have time for family and friends? Are they workaholics who neglect the proper relaxation of mind and body? An honest answer to these and other related questions will, I believe, indicate to them whether they are keeping the Lord's day holy in the sense that God intended.

7. Are Distractions in Prayer Normal?

Dear Father,

I made a weekend retreat this year. Since then, I've been trying to say extra prayers, but mostly I experience extra distractions. They give me a lot of trouble at Mass and in my personal prayers. Maybe you could say something about this topic.

Kim

Dear Kim,

Any person who takes his or her prayer life seriously is going to be troubled at times about distractions. This is clear from the lives of the saints. Almost every saint who wrote about the spiritual life gives advice about handling distractions in prayer. In a moment I'll mention a few of their suggestions.

But first, what is meant by a distraction? A distraction may be defined as the movement of the mind from one particular train of thought to another; a shifting of attention from one object to another or to several different objects at the same time. A distraction at prayer means a shifting of the attention from the Lord to some other person or object.

It's clear from this definition that a distraction at prayer may be voluntary or involuntary. It is *voluntary* when a person freely and willingly chooses to shift his or her attention from the Lord to some other person or object. Such a choice is obviously a sign of disrespect to God. It is sinful. It renders prayer fruitless.

It is *involuntary* when no matter how hard a person tries, his or her mind wanders from the presence of God to other thoughts. One usually becomes aware of this all of a sudden: "I started my night prayers, earnestly and sincerely, and all of a sudden I realized I was planning tomorrow's dinner or replaying yesterday's tennis match."

It's important to realize that such involuntary distractions are part of the human condition. For all practical purposes, they are inescapable. They are due to the way the mind and imagination actually function. There is no complete "automatic" control over them. In dealing with such involuntary distractions, it's important to be patient.

The saints offer some good suggestions for those who suffer from distractions. Saint Theresa, one of the foremost teachers of prayer, says they should try to begin their prayer with a deep Act of Faith in the presence of God. This starting point is extremely significant. It is a way for people to "change gears" from what they have been doing to what they want to do now. It is a turning away from other concerns and a focusing on the Lord.

Even with such a good start, however, distractions may still arise. When people become aware of them, Saint Theresa says, they should quietly and calmly renew their Act of Faith and continue their prayer. They should remember that no matter how often distractions return or how prolonged they might be, they are not sinful or displeasing to God. They are, in fact, extra opportunities to prove that pray-ers really want to pray and that they will persevere in prayer even though these distractions make it difficult.

Saint Alphonsus Liguori, another great teacher of prayer, points out that one of the common pitfalls even for good persons is discouragement in the face of distractions. They begin to doubt their sincerity — even thinking about giving up their prayer life — when they seem overwhelmed with distractions. But Saint Alphonsus warns that this kind of discouragement plays into the hands of the devil, who would like nothing more than to have people stop praying!

To summarize, Kim: If your distractions are voluntary, you have to stop playing games and get serious about your relationship with the Lord. If your distractions are involuntary, you should try to start your prayer as well as you can, calmly return to the Lord when you become aware of distractions, and above all, never quit praying, no matter how often these distractions return.

8. Are Laypeople Called to Holiness?

Dear Father,

Ever since I was a little girl I've been interested in what it means to be holy. I am now the mother of three young children. I don't have much time for prayer and meditation — especially quiet meditation! What can I do to bring holiness into my life?

Liz

Dear Liz,

When you ponder the Scriptures and listen to the advice of the saints — your models of holiness — you come to the conclusion that holiness means, above all, the love of God. You also begin to see that the love of God has two basic dimensions: first, God's great love for you; and, second, your love for God in return.

Like the sun that rises unbidden each morning to warm the earth, God's love is freely lavished on all persons. His love is poured out upon them, not because they have proven themselves worthy of it, but because they are the "apple of his eye." The evangelist John writes: "We love because he first loved us" (1 John 4:19). This "first love" of God is unconditional and unlimited. This love, more than anything else, makes people holy. It is vital that they appreciate God's overwhelming love for them. If they do not, they will find no motivation to love God in return. Yet sadly, as Henri Nouwen laments, "Few people know that they are loved without any conditions or limits" (*In the Name of Jesus: Reflections on Christian Leadership in the Future,* Crossroad Publishing Company, page 18).

This love of God for his creatures deserves a response on their part. But how can they respond to God's love? There are, to be sure, many ways; but one of the main ones is the way featured by Jesus himself: "Everything that the Father gives me will come to me, and I will not reject anyone who comes to me, because I came down from heaven not to do my own will but the will of the one who sent me" (John 6:37-38).

Of his disciples, Jesus said: "Whoever does the will of my heavenly Father is my brother, and sister, and mother" (Matthew 12:50). Echoing this gospel principle, Saint Alphonsus Liguori, one of the great theologians in the Church's history, developed a basic summary, a kind of syllogism, concerning the proper response to God:

All holiness consists in the love of God;
But the love of God consists in conformity
   to the will of God;
Therefore, all holiness consists in conformity
   to the will of God.

From this point of view, holiness means trying to know and to do the will of God in life. How is God's will manifested? Principally, of course, through the Scriptures, the living Word of God, and through the Church, guided by the Spirit to teach in matters of faith and morals. Further, however, the will of God is manifested to us in the duties and responsibilities of a person's vocation in life — and very concretely, in the peculiar circumstances of his or her life here and now.

This latter point is extremely important, Liz. Sometimes you may think of holiness as "out there" instead of "down here." As a wife and a mother, here and now, holiness for you can be found in loving your husband, patiently raising your children, building good family relationships, preparing meals, arranging birthday parties, looking for mittens…and doing the thousand and one "services" that are part of your present life. If you make all of these part of your loving response to God, you are on the path to holiness.

It is not always easy to accept this teaching of the saints. Many persons, I believe, have been exposed to a kind of split view of life: namely, that there are "holy" things (like prayer and meditation) and "worldly" things (like preparing meals and playing with children). In truth, holiness embraces your total human existence: prayer and family life and work and recreation.

How do you, Liz, become holy in your chosen vocation in life? By believing in God's unconditional love for you and by living every moment of your life in loving response to that love.

9. Should I Be More Involved in the Church?

Dear Father,

I feel there's more I should be doing in the Church, but I don't know what. This makes me feel guilty. I've done some things for a right-to-life group, and last Easter I was a sponsor for someone who was baptized, but it still doesn't seem as if I've done enough.

Mary Lou

Dear Mary Lou,

I believe you are one of a growing number of Catholics who recognize that you have a positive role to play in the mission of the Church. I congratulate you. I'm sure there are still a large number of Catholics who are satisfied with attending Mass on Saturday evening or Sunday morning — and that's it for their Catholic lives! But fortunately, this mind-set seems to be changing.

It is abundantly clear both from the gospel and from the teaching of the Church that each baptized person is called to build the kingdom of God. The kingdom cannot be built by "religious professionals" alone. It needs the talent, time, and energy of every baptized person.

Pope Paul VI, shortly before he died, issued his magnificent letter to the whole Church with the title *On Evangelization.* In that letter the Pope points out that all baptized Christians share in the mission of Christ himself and that their mission is evangelization. What is this evangelization? "To evangelize means to bring the Gospel into all levels of society, and through its influence to transform humankind from within and make it new...."

This work of evangelization can and must be done in many different ways: witnessing to gospel values in your family, your job, your neighborhood, your secular group, your Church. I cannot tell you exactly and precisely what you should be doing, but I would like to offer you a few points for reflection.

First, what part you play in evangelization or in building the kingdom of God depends in large measure on your present relationships and responsibilities. The working parents of four young children, for example, will probably not have much time or energy for other works of charity outside the home. They certainly should not feel guilty about this. They are doing God's work and building the kingdom of their own family. Fifteen years from now, however, these same parents may have a lot of time and energy to devote to community groups and the community of the Church. At that time they should be ready to reevaluate their part in building the kingdom of God.

Second, to help you in your present dilemma, I would recommend what some spiritual writers call "the process of discerning God's will." This means that you calmly and prayerfully examine your life — your present responsibilities and commitments, your talents, your health, your free time — in relationship to the concrete demands that a more active role in the Church would place upon you.

In working through this process, it is usually helpful to make a list of pros and cons. For example, if I give one evening a week to right-to-life work, will I have to sacrifice some other activity? How important is this other activity? Then pray over the list, discuss it with a spiritual director or wise friend, and patiently wait for the Lord to provide light.

I believe, Mary Lou, that every Catholic — young or old, healthy or disabled, married or single — can do something to witness to the gospel and to build God's kingdom here and now. It may be a project quite limited as far as time and energy are concerned, or it may be one that is quite extensive. I want to encourage you to keep looking for something that fits your life now. And do this not out of a sense of guilt, but as your positive contribution to building the kingdom!

---

10. What Is a Retreat?

Dear Father,

In our parish every year there are several announcements about weekend retreats open to men and women of the parish. Our pastor strongly encourages people to sign up for these retreats. I have not always been a practicing Catholic and I am now playing catch-up on Catholic terms and ideas. What is a retreat? Why do people go on a retreat?

Jan

Dear Jan,

I was happy to receive your letter, mainly because I am now on the staff of a Catholic retreat center near Milwaukee, Wisconsin. Our entire ministry is dedicated to retreats. Most dioceses have one or more retreat centers similar to ours.

If you were to look up the word *retreat* in your dictionary, you would find that the first meaning of the word emphasizes withdrawal from something that is difficult or dangerous, for example, the forced withdrawal of troops from enemy forces. In the religious use of the word, this idea of withdrawal is also present. A religious retreat is a withdrawal from one's routine life and work in order to reflect on, discuss, and pray about one's way of life, one's problems, one's relationship with God.

Retreats have a long history in the Catholic community, going back to the days when men and women would go to the desert to find solitude and peace of mind in a special encounter with God. The Church has always considered retreats an important way to deepen one's relationship with God and to renew one's living of the Christian life. Priests and members of religious communities are required by the law of the Church to make some days of retreat each year. Thousands of laypeople, too, spend some days in retreat each year. They would never miss their annual retreat because they believe it is this spiritual renewal that brings so much happiness and peace to their lives.

In the Church today, there are many different kinds of retreats. There are weekend, midweek, and even monthlong retreats. Some emphasize complete silence and solitude; others stress community, sharing, and dialogue among the retreatants. Preached retreats feature the presentation of the Word of God by the retreat director to the assembled group. Directed retreats usually imply a one-on-one encounter between the retreatant and the spiritual director. Retreats are commonly designed for particular age groups, such as teenagers or senior citizens and for particular states in life, such as priests, single laypersons, married couples, the widowed, the divorced. There are retreats available for everybody!

Why do people go on a retreat? I would say, Jan, that there are almost as many reasons as there are people! For many people it is a special time to reflect on their relationship with God and those with whom they live and work and play; it is a time to "take inventory" of their Christian life and to renew their spirit. Other people make a retreat only occasionally. It may be that they are experiencing a need to "get away from it all," a need for some quiet time of reflection and relaxation. Or they may be facing important decisions in their lives and want to seek the Lord's guidance. Some people make a retreat because they are seeking solutions to personal problems or trying to settle religious doubts.

From my experience, Jan, I would say that many persons who have never before made a retreat usually begin their first one with some hesitation and fear. That is certainly understandable. After all, they don't know what they are getting into, and fear of the unknown is one of the most common of all fears! Yet I would say that almost all end a retreat with a certain measure of joy, peace, and happiness. There is something very enriching about taking time out with the Lord to look at your life and to get your priorities in order. I hope someday you will give it a try, Jan.

11. How Should a Person Prepare for Death?

Dear Father,

I have cancer. The medical experts do not give me much hope of recovery. I am only forty-four. I am at times angry at God and afraid of the future. At other times I wish that death would come quickly. I do not know what to make of my feelings. I do not know how to face death. Can you help me?

Tim

Dear Tim,

You are not alone in your excruciating dilemma. In today's society, people hardly ever speak honestly and directly about death. They use all kinds of euphemisms to cloak its harsh reality. Therefore, it is not surprising that you do not know how to face death.

I have been helped in my own reflections on this topic by the writings of Dr. Elisabeth Kubler-Ross, who for some twenty-five years has been trying to help those who are dying and those who keep vigil with them. In her book *On Death and Dying* (Macmillan, 1970), she outlines five stages in the dying process. She does not mean that these are neat and orderly steps through which every dying person walks. It is not a question of going to stage one, finishing it, and then proceeding to stage two. Rather, Tim, these stages indicate the various feelings and emotions many people experience as they face the inevitability of death. Thinking about these stages may help you sort out your own feelings.

The first stage is *denial.* In effect, the dying person tries to believe that the physician has made a mistake, that the seriousness of the illness has been misdiagnosed, that all will turn out fine. Often enough, friends and relatives contribute to this denial because they themselves do not want to talk about the reality of death. I gather from your letter, Tim, that you have moved beyond this stage.

The second stage is *anger.* Most commonly this anger is directed toward God. For younger persons especially, the anger settles around the plaintive questions "Why me? Why is God doing this to me?" In your letter you say that you are "at times angry at God." I think it is important to know that God understands your feelings of anger. It is okay for you to tell God how you feel. He will not turn away from you. He knows you better than you know yourself. As in life, so in death, the Lord will always be there for you.

A third stage is *bargaining*. Here the dying person admits his or her condition but then tries to strike bargains with God. "If I am spared, I promise that I will always do such and such" or "I will never again do such and such." This is an understandable human reaction made by many at one time or another in their lives. Yet it is also a doomed strategy because it cannot keep death at bay.

The fourth stage is *depression*. This would seem to be almost inevitable. After all, the dying person is about to lose all that he or she has ever known or loved: life, laughter, relationships. It is only natural to grieve over the prospect of such loss. While depression is natural and understandable, it can also be devastating. Blessed are they who have help in dealing with their depression as death draws near.

The final stage is *acceptance*. For some people this stage comes only at the very end, if at all. For others it comes early in the dying process, and that is a great blessing indeed. Acceptance does not necessarily imply joy or elation, but it does imply the peaceful realization that "my hour has come, my life is done, I am ready to go."

It seems to me, Tim, that this is where your faith can really come to your aid. The saints recommend going beyond the stage of acceptance to a full and free embracing of God's holy will, even if you do not understand it. Saint Alphonsus Liguori prayed often in his life: "I will what God wills: when he wills it, as he wills it, because he wills it." In a privately printed *Way of the Cross,* which I often use, there is this beautiful prayer for the twelfth station (Jesus dies on the cross): "My Lord Jesus, you laid down your life for me. I shall lay down my life for you. I offer you my death with all the pain that may surround it, accepting at this moment, whatever kind of death you have in store for me. I give you my life and my death, my body and soul, my whole being now and forever."

I pray, Tim, that this will become your prayer too.

12. What Must I Believe About Purgatory?

Dear Father,

In the mail I received some material that described purgatory in very frightening and horrible terms. This material is supposed to be from private revelations to saintly people. I was very upset by it and wish I had not received it. Am I obliged to believe such writings?

Dennis

Dear Dennis,

In answering your letter, it might be helpful to touch on two points: first, private revelations in general, and second, private revelations about purgatory.

Concerning private revelations, it is well known that the Church's attitude toward them is one of utmost caution. The reason for this caution — and here the Church has vast experience — is the great danger of illusion, error, and even fraud. At any given moment, there are a number of people in various parts of the world claiming personal revelations from God, from Mary, or from one of the saints. It is understandable that the Church does not accept these at face value. If a particular private revelation seems to be worthy of further attention, the Church will investigate further.

If thorough examination shows that particular private revelations are in accord with divine revelation and Catholic teaching, and if the danger of illusion or fraud is reasonably excluded, the Church may then give her approval. This implies that there is nothing contrary to true faith in them and that the faithful may accept them in a prudent way. Even when the Church gives its limited approval, however, the Catholic faithful are not obliged to believe these revelations.

Concerning purgatory, the authentic teaching of the Church is direct and simple: Purgatory does exist — not for the damned but for the elect (those who have died in the state of grace, that is, as friends of God); and it consists of purification from the temporal punishment still due to sins committed during life. The Church does not give any detailed information about the nature of this purification. A good example of the Church's official teaching was stated at the Council of Lyons (1274): "If those who are truly repentant die in charity before they have done sufficient penance for their sins of omission and commission, their souls are cleansed after death in purgatorial or cleansing punishments."

But the private revelations about purgatory — and there have been many of them in the Church's history — are by no means direct and simple! Many of them have been characterized by curiosity, superstition, and exaggeration.

In 1979 the Sacred Congregation for the Doctrine of the Faith issued a *Letter on Certain Questions Concerning Eschatology* and reminded the bishops of the world: "When dealing with man's situation after death, one must especially beware of arbitrary imaginative representations: Excess of this kind is a major cause of the difficulties that Christian faith often encounters.... We must provide the faithful with the means to be firm with regard to the essence of the doctrine and at the same time careful not to allow childish or arbitrary images to be considered truths of faith." It seems clear to me, Dennis, that the type of material you have received (and I've received it too) is full of "arbitrary imaginative representations."

This same document affirmed that "the Church believes in the possibility of a purification for the elect before they see God, a purification altogether different from the punishment of the damned." That phrase "altogether different from the punishment of the damned" should be underlined. Some of the private writings on purgatory seem to describe it as the equivalent of hell. Such a description is not in accord with the teaching of the Church.

To be sure, both the teaching and practice of the Church urge Catholics to pray for those in purgatory, that their time of purification will be brief. Each year on November 2, the Church celebrates All Souls' Day and offers special prayers for all the faithful departed. But it should not be forgotten that by God's grace those in purgatory have already achieved salvation. What every Catholic hopes for, they have achieved: They have died as friends of God and are assured of heaven.

By way of summary, Dennis, my answer to your question is this: As a Catholic you are not obliged to believe private revelations of any kind, and you should certainly reject out of hand those that contradict or confuse the authentic teaching of the Church on purgatory.

13. Does Hell Exist?

Dear Father,
I have a friend, a Catholic married woman, who denies the existence of hell. She says that God is all-merciful and that our hell is here on earth. I told her that hell is spoken of in the Bible and that the Catholic Church has a definite teaching about hell. Who is right?

Doris

Dear Doris,

You are certainly right in saying that hell is spoken of in the Bible and that the Catholic Church has a definite teaching about it. At the same time, your friend is right in putting her finger on the troubling question of the relationship between the mercy and justice of God.

The word *hell* (which seems to come from an old German word) is not used in the Bible, but other words that carry the same meaning are used often. For example, *Gehenna* is used eleven times in the Synoptic Gospels. Gehenna was a valley to the south of Jerusalem where there was a smoldering dump, a place where fire burned continually. (See Isaiah 66:24.)

Jesus uses this image in his preaching. "If your hand causes you to sin, cut it off. It is better for you to enter into life maimed than with two hands to go into Gehenna, into the unquenchable fire" (Mark 9:43). Another example: "And do not be afraid of those who kill the body but cannot kill the soul; rather, be afraid of one who can destroy both soul and body in Gehenna" (Matthew 10:28).

Saint Paul, too, often expresses the idea of eternal punishment, emphasizing how it banishes the evil from the face of God. Speaking of "those who do not acknowledge God" and "those who do not obey the gospel of our Lord Jesus," Paul asserts: "These will pay the penalty of eternal ruin, separated from the presence of the Lord and from the glory of his power, when he comes to be glorified among his holy ones..." (2 Thessalonians 1:9-10).

Drawing upon the teaching of the New Testament, the Church from its earliest days taught the doctrine of eternal reward and eternal punishment (heaven and hell). In the Athanasian Creed (from about A.D. 400), the Church proclaims: "At his [Christ's] coming, all are to arise with their own bodies; and they are to give an account of their lives. Those who have done good deeds will go into eternal life; those who have done evil will go into everlasting fire."

This same teaching was reaffirmed just a few years ago: "In fidelity to the New Testament and tradition, the Church believes in...the doctrine of hell: that is, the eternal punishment of the unrepentant sinner, a punishment that will have a repercussion on the whole being of the sinner, who will be deprived of the sight of God" (Congregation for the Doctrine of the Faith, *Letter on Certain Questions Concerning Eschatology,* 1979).

Though there are many imaginative descriptions of hell in literature (notably in Dante's *Divine Comedy*), the Church has never given us a complete or detailed description of it. While Catholic teaching affirms that hell involves some "pain of the senses," usually described as "fire," the primary punishment of hell is the inexpressible "pain of loss": the deprivation of the face-to-face vision of God and eternal happiness with him. Grave sin is a turning away from God, an estrangement from him. It is a free and deliberate choice of isolation and separation from God and others. To die in the state of grave sin is to choose absolute isolation.

Perhaps, Doris, this is the point that your friend needs to think about. It is true, as I mentioned above, that the doctrine of hell raises profound questions about the relationship between God's mercy and his justice. Yet these questions must always be considered in the light of human freedom. "The possibility of hell," writes Zachary Hayes, O.F.M., "cannot be denied without denying human freedom itself" (*The New Dictionary of Theology*, Michael Glazier, Inc., page 459).

The existence of hell is a sign of how completely God respects human freedom and choice. It is not so much God imposing a punishment as it is the sinner choosing his or her own punishment, and God respecting that choice. God has created people free to seek him or reject him. If they radically reject him, they open the door of hell for themselves.

Thomas Merton has insightfully written about this paradox: "Our God also is a consuming fire. And if we, by love, become transformed into him and burn as he burns, his fire will be our everlasting joy. But if we refuse his love and remain in the coldness of sin and opposition to him and to other men, then will his fire (by our own choice rather than his) become our everlasting enemy, and love, instead of being our joy, will become our torment and our destruction" (*New Seeds of Contemplation*, New Direction Books, page 124).

It is worth stressing, Doris, that while the Church declares the canonized saints to be in heaven, the Church has never asserted that any particular individual person is actually in hell. The Church keeps hoping and praying, in the words of John Paul II, "that very few persist to the end in this attitude of rebellion or even defiance of God." The Scriptures constantly proclaim that the Lord is rich in mercy and the Church constantly extends that mercy to all men and women. Hell is only for those who adamantly refuse to accept the mercy of God.

14. What Does the Church Teach About Heaven?

Dear Father,

I am seventy-two. I have been a Catholic all my life. Heaven is supposed to be our final goal, yet I can count on one hand the number of sermons I have heard on this topic in recent years. Why don't Catholic preachers speak of it more often? What does the Church teach about heaven?

Melba

Dear Melba,

It may seem odd to you, but even well-trained preachers and teachers find it hard to talk about heaven. After all, they have no direct knowledge or experience of it. They know that the life of heaven is a radically new and different form of existence, beyond human grasp, knowable only through the Spirit.

> "What eye has not seen, and ear has not heard,
>   and what has not entered the human heart,
>   what God has prepared for those who love him,"
> this God has revealed to us through the Spirit.

(1 Corinthians 2:9-10)

Because of these limitations, heaven tends to be pictured in mostly materialistic images: pearly gates, streets lined with gold, a life of ease and comfort, and the like. This is strange because Biblical and Christian Tradition present heaven in metaphors and comparisons that are more spiritual and relational. These images depict interpersonal relationships with God and others, with the absence of pain and sorrow, with the fullness of life.

For example, the New Testament describes the glory of heaven as the face-to-face vision of God. "Beloved, we are God's children now; what we shall be has not yet been revealed. We do know that when it is revealed we shall be like him, for we shall see him as he is" (1 John 3:2). Or again: "We see indistinctly, as in a mirror, but then face to face. At present I know partially; then I shall know fully, as I am fully known" (1 Corinthians 13:12).

This face-to-face vision of God is called, in the formal teaching of the Church, the "beatific vision." Those in heaven shall see the very essence of God in all his beauty and goodness; and in this marvelous vision, they will know and love God forever.

The Scriptures also describe heaven as the dwelling place of God and the angels and saints and the place of eternal happiness of all those who have been saved. "Then I saw a new heaven and a new earth....I heard a loud voice from the throne saying, 'Behold, God's dwelling is with the human race. He will dwell with them and they will be his people and God himself will always be with them [as their God]. He will wipe every tear from their eyes, and there shall be no more death or mourning, wailing or pain, [for] the old order has passed away' " (Revelation 21:1, 3-4).

Saint Thomas Aquinas, probably the greatest theologian the Church has even known, put a "human touch" on the happiness of heaven. "Eternal life consists of the joyous community of all the blessed, a community of supreme delight, since everyone will share all that is good with all the blessed. Everyone will love everyone else as himself, and therefore will rejoice in another's good as in his own. So it follows that the happiness and joy of each grows in proportion to the joy of all."

According to Catholic teaching, Melba, heaven is perfect love: love without limitation, without imperfection, without end. Heaven is fullness of life: without illness, without strife, without death. To be sure, you have never experienced such love and life. Perhaps that is why Saint Augustine reminded all God's children that whatever is found beautiful or desirable in this world is but a faint reflection of God.

In the course of your life, Melba, you experience some powerful hints of love and beauty and happiness. These hints can enable you to imagine what the happiness of heaven will be like when you are in the presence of God, who is love and surrounded by a loving community. Above all, they can inspire you to desire and strive for your final goal of heaven.

You are certainly right, Melba, in asking why the Church doesn't preach more about heaven. You should hear more about it. It's the best news you'll ever hear.

PART II

MORAL QUESTIONS

15. Do People Who Commit Suicide Go to Hell?

Dear Father,

Recently, my brother committed suicide. The priest of his parish was very understanding and had a funeral Mass for Bill. Yet I was brought up with the idea that suicide is a great sin and that people who committed suicide went to hell. Is this true? Also, I feel guilty about my brother's death. I tried to help him by getting him to go for professional counseling. Why do I feel so guilty?

Gary

Dear Gary,

I extend my sympathy to you on the death of your brother. I hope that my answer to your letter will be of some consolation to you.

First, I would like to explain briefly a distinction that is very important in any Catholic understanding of morality. I refer to the distinction between objective and subjective morality.

Objective morality refers to the nature of the act, to what is actually done. In this case, it is suicide or the taking of one's own life. Objectively, according to Catholic teaching, suicide is morally wrong. "Intentionally causing one's own death, or suicide, is therefore equally as wrong as murder; such an action on the part of a person is to be considered as a rejection of God's sovereignty and loving plan. Furthermore, suicide is also often a refusal of love for self, the denial of the natural instinct to live, a flight from the duties of justice and charity owed to one's neighbor" (Congregation for the Doctrine of the Faith, *Declaration on Euthanasia,* 1980, #3). In the Christian Tradition, as you were taught, Gary, suicide has always been considered morally wrong.

Subjective morality, on the other hand, refers to the mental and psychological state of the person who committed a given act. Was that person responsible for an objectively immoral act? Did that person act knowingly and freely? In this regard, Catholic moral teaching recognizes that suicide is often performed without sufficient deliberation or freedom to warrant subjective guilt. Many suicides are due to profound psychological disturbances or mental imbalances. These factors can be so strong as to severely diminish or even completely remove moral responsibility.

I hope what I am saying does not appear to be double-talk, Gary. Catholic teaching does indeed consider suicide a serious violation of God's law; but, at the same time, does not presume to judge the personal responsibility of those who commit suicide. Judgment belongs to the Lord, to no one else. The Church practices what it preaches: "Do not make any judgment before the appointed time, until the Lord comes, for he will bring to light what is hidden in darkness and will manifest the motives of our hearts" (1 Corinthians 4:5). Do people who commit suicide go to hell? It certainly should not be presumed that they do. Their judgment should be prayerfully left in the hands of a merciful God.

In regard to your feelings of guilt, Gary, there is another helpful distinction, namely, the one between true guilt and false guilt. True guilt is a state of mind or soul that follows upon a personal, free, and deliberate transgression of God's law. Theologian Sean Fagan emphasizes that true guilt "is the experience of conscience making its judgment in the light of rationally evaluated circumstances and recognizing that it has done wrong" (*New Dictionary of Theology,* Michael Glazier, Inc., page 452). This awareness that one has done wrong gives rise to "guilt feelings," that is, feelings of spiritual unrest that seek relief. Guilt feelings urge the sinful person to repent and to seek reconciliation and thus once again to experience inner peace.

In contrast to true guilt which follows upon actual sin, false guilt (also called abnormal or neurotic guilt) seems to arise from an exaggerated sense of responsibility or from a vague conviction that "I have done wrong; I always do wrong." It is, to quote Sean Fagan again, "a state of emotional disturbance unrelated to any wrongdoing" (*ibidem*, page 451). For many people false guilt is a relic from childhood training. It can be persistent and devastating. I believe, Gary, that you are suffering from false guilt. You did what you could for your brother. You did what any expert would advise you to do: You urged your brother to get professional counseling. For the rest, you must "let go and let God." I know that it is painful to think that you let your brother down. But what more could you have done? Please do not torture yourself over something that you could not control.

16. Is Capital Punishment Right or Wrong?

Dear Father,
    Is the death penalty "murder by society"? Our priest says the Old Testament taught "An eye for an eye," but in the New Testament, Jesus preached, "Turn the other

*cheek." I'm confused. What are the views of the Catholic
Church regarding capital punishment?*

Debbie

Dear Debbie,

I suppose you are not the only person of conscience confused
about capital punishment. It's a very real problem. I don't think
it helps much to quote Scripture verses back and forth. There is
no definitive teaching about capital punishment in the Scriptures.
As with so many other realities in life (such as self-defense and
war), Christians had to try to come to a correct moral position by
using right reason in the light of Biblical teaching.

For many centuries Christian teaching has accepted in principle that the state (legitimate public authority) has the right to
take the life of a person guilty of very serious ("capital") crimes.
This did not mean that the state had to use this right. In fact, many
national constitutions forbade the use of this right. Even today the
United States is one of the few major nations of the world that
allows capital punishment. (The Supreme Court of the United
States reinstated the death penalty in 1976. From that time until
late 1990, one hundred and forty-two persons have been executed.)

Among Catholics, then, the question is not so much about the
right of the state to impose capital punishment but whether capital
punishment is morally justifiable in the concrete circumstances
of modern society. In other words, should it actually be used?
Here, there is a lot of disagreement. Some Catholics, as other
citizens, believe that capital punishment is definitely morally
justifiable. According to some opinion polls I have seen, the
majority of Americans, including Catholics, are in favor of capital
punishment. Others, however, are strongly opposed to capital
punishment and believe it should be completely abolished. I
believe it is fair to say that this is the position of the leadership of
the Catholic Church. I refer specifically to Pope John Paul II and
to the United States Catholic Bishops.

It has long been the teaching of Christian ethics that punishment of any kind, since it involves the deliberate infliction of evil on another person, needs justification. The three justifications for punishment traditionally given are

1. Reform: This consists of rehabilitating the criminal and restoring him or her to a productive place in society.
2. Deterrence: This implies a forewarning of others who might be tempted to commit the same kind of crime.
3. Retribution: This demands the reestablishment of the balance of justice in society, vindicating the rights of the offended.

Now, how do these justifications fit in regard to capital punishment?

The first justification, reform, can be ruled out immediately, since no rehabilitation is possible once a person has been put to death.

Deterrence, the second justification for capital punishment, does not really prevent further crime, according to the United States Catholic Bishops. In the decade of the eighties, they frequently expressed their moral opposition to capital punishment, maintaining that deterrence has a doubtful effect: "Empirical studies in this area have not given conclusive evidence that would justify the imposition of the death penalty on a few individuals as a means of preventing others from committing crimes. There are strong reasons to doubt that many crimes of violence are undertaken in a spirit of rational calculation which would be influenced by a remote threat of death" (*Statement on Capital Punishment,* 1980, #6).

Retribution, the third justification, is not the answer either. The United States Catholic Bishops agree that certain forms of retribution are justified, but not capital punishment: "We grant that the need for retribution does indeed justify punishment. For the practice of punishment both presupposes a previous transgression against the law and involves the involuntary deprivation of certain goods. But we maintain that this need does not require nor does it justify taking the life of the criminal, even in cases of murder" (*ibidem*, #8).

The United States Catholic Bishops offer "serious considerations" which they believe should encourage all Americans to oppose capital punishment. Among these considerations are "the evils present in the practice of capital punishment." These evils include the possibility of mistake, the generation of unhealthy publicity, unfair discrimination against the poor and members of minorities, and long delays and appeals that diminish the effect on other criminals and cause deep anxiety to the condemned and his or her family.

These same bishops have also stressed "important values" that would be fostered by the abolition of capital punishment. Among these values would be a renewed appreciation that human life at every stage is sacred and that God alone is the Lord of life.

Each of these points could be developed and argued, Debbie, but even the simple statement of them may help you and others make up your mind about the morality of capital punishment in today's society.

---

17. Why Is the Catholic Church So Opposed to Abortion?

Dear Father,

My wife is Catholic, I am not. I consider myself an ethical person, and I am not in favor of the widespread practice of abortion in our society. I think there could be a middle ground, but this does not sit well with Catholics. Why is the Catholic Church so absolutely opposed to abortion?

Conrad

Dear Conrad,

I'm afraid that in this short space I cannot say all that should be said in response to your courteous letter. I would like, however, to touch on several important points.

First, your letter seems to imply that opposition to abortion is a "Catholic issue," as if only the Catholic Church is adamantly opposed to it. This is not true. Many other Churches are equally opposed. Moreover, there are individuals with no religious affiliation at all who also stand strongly opposed to abortion.

Second, you suggest that there could be a "middle ground" on abortion. Unfortunately, I do not know in detail what your understanding of abortion is. The Catholic Church's understanding of abortion, as I shall show in a moment, makes a "middle ground" quite impossible.

Third, what exactly is the position of the Catholic Church on abortion? I believe that this position is carefully spelled out in two documents: (1) the Vatican's *Declaration on Procured Abortion,* 1976; and (2) the formal statement of the United States Catholic Bishops, *To Live in Christ Jesus: A Pastoral Reflection on the Moral Life,* 1976.

From the *Declaration on Procured Abortion:*
Respect for human life is called for from the time that the process of generation begins. From the time that the ovum is fertilized, a life is begun which is neither that of the father nor of the mother; it is rather the life of a new human being with his or her own growth. It would never be made human if it were not already....Divine law and natural reason, therefore, exclude all right to the direct killing of an innocent human person.

From *To Live in Christ Jesus:*
Every human life is inviolable from its very beginning. While the unborn child may not be aware of itself and its

rights, it is a human entity, a human being with potential, not a potential human being. Like the newborn, the unborn depend on others for life and the opportunity to share human goods....To destroy these innocent unborn children is an unspeakable crime, a crime which subordinates weaker members of the human community to the interest of the stronger... (#63-64).

I have to admit, Conrad, that these statements touch me deeply, not only because I am a Catholic but also because they ring true with all that human reason and experience have taught me. I don't know how you react to the above descriptions, but I think you will immediately recognize that if you did agree with them, you would see that there could be no middle ground on the abortion issue.

The Catholic Church understands abortion to be the direct killing of an innocent human person and therefore "an unspeakable crime." How can there be any middle ground on this? Can it be said that it's morally right to kill an innocent human person during the first three months of pregnancy but not right during the last three months? How is it possible to say such a thing? The Catholic Church is absolutely opposed to abortion because it is always morally wrong. In a matter of such vital importance, the Catholic Church has no other choice.

I know, of course, that many Americans believe that somehow the life of the unborn child belongs to the mother. One of the clichés in the abortion debate is that "a woman should have rights over her own body." But should she also have rights over the life of an innocent human being growing in her body — "a human being with potential, not a potential human being"? Who gives her those rights? Where do they come from? How can the Supreme Court or any other human organization give one person the right over another person's life?

Today's society is plagued, Conrad, by a profound lack of

respect for human life at all stages. I am afraid that abortion is merely the tip of the iceberg. Once the most helpless of all human beings is deprived of the right to life, what will prevent others who are also helpless from losing their right to life? The "slippery slope" will keep getting slipperier. It always does. As an ethical man, Conrad, you might find cause for great concern here.

18. What Is the Church's Position on Artificial Fertilization?

Dear Father,

My wife and I were the only Catholics at a social gathering. A heated argument broke out about a story in the local paper saying that the Catholic Church condemned all forms of artificial fertilization. We were challenged to "defend" the Church's "negative" position. Sorry to say, we didn't even know what the Church's position is. Can you fill us in?

Phil

Dear Phil,

The story in your local paper was no doubt about the Vatican's wide-ranging *Instruction on Respect for Human Life in Its Origins* issued in 1987. That *Instruction* dealt with the morality of "artificial fertilization." This term refers to various technical procedures aimed at obtaining a human conception in a manner other than the sexual union of husband and wife. In my reply to your request, Phil, I would like to indicate the Church's position on three forms of artificial fertilization.

One form of artificial fertilization occurs when a human conception is brought about by transferring into the woman's genital tract sperm previously collected from a donor other than her husband. This "donor insemination" received quite a bit of attention in the 1940s. In 1949 Pope Pius XII addressed this issue. He wrote: "Artificial insemination in marriage, but produced by the active element of a third party is…immoral and as such to be condemned outright." He went on to explain that the marriage act is a "personal and cooperative act on the part of husband and wife…much more than the union of seeds brought about artificially, without the natural and personal act of husband and wife."

In the above-mentioned *Instruction,* the same judgment is repeated; namely, that "the fertilization of a married woman with the sperm of a donor different from her husband…is morally illicit." This *Instruction* insists that "artificial fertilization by donor is contrary to the unity of marriage, to the dignity of the spouses, to the vocation proper to parents, and to the child's right to be conceived and brought into the world in marriage and from marriage."

Upon reflection, Phil, you can see how the presence of a third party (donor) in the conception of a child somehow violates the essential and necessary relationship in the areas of human sexuality, marriage, and parenthood. The child conceived through artificial fertilization by donor is deprived of any moral or legal relationship with his or her parental origins. This child is not the child of a known married couple and is not a member of an integral family.

A second form of artificial fertilization is commonly referred to as "surrogate motherhood." This term refers to two separate cases. In the first case the woman carries in pregnancy an embryo implanted in her uterus through the union of ovum and sperm from "donors." She pledges to surrender the baby to the party who commissioned or made the agreement for the pregnancy.

In the second case the woman carries in pregnancy an embryo to whose procreation she has contributed the donation of her own ovum, which is fertilized through insemination with the sperm of a man other than her husband. As in the first case, she conceives the pregnancy with a pledge to surrender the baby to the party who commissioned or made the agreement for the pregnancy.

You are probably familiar, Phil, with news reports on the legal and social complexities of surrogate motherhood, raising questions like these: To whom does this child really belong? How binding is the pledge to give up the child? These and many other questions lead one to wonder about the morality of surrogate motherhood.

The 1987 Vatican *Instruction* asks this very question: Is surrogate motherhood morally licit? The answer is given in these words: "No, for the same reasons which lead one to reject artificial fertilization by donor: for it is contrary to the unity of marriage and to the dignity of the human person." This basic conviction of the immorality of surrogate motherhood is shared by many moralists, Catholic and non-Catholic alike. Among the many reasons given are the following:

Surrogate motherhood violates the marriage covenant between husband and wife; dehumanizes the procreative process; exploits women, especially those who take money for the use of their bodies; treats the child as a mere commodity; subverts the child's relationship with his or her mother; disguises the child's true ancestry.

A third form of artificial fertilization takes place within marriage, that is, between husband and wife. This can be carried out by two different methods: (1) a technique whereby a human conception is brought about *in vitro* (that is, in a test tube): The ovum is fertilized by the sperm with resulting embryo implanted in the uterus for gestation; or (2) a bringing about of human conception through the transfer into the genital tract of a married woman the sperm previously collected from her husband.

What is the morality of such artificial fertilization within marriage? According to the 1987 *Instruction,* both of these methods are morally wrong. There are three basic reasons given for this moral position. In brief outline they are as follows:

First, there is the fundamental moral principle taught by Pope Paul VI concerning the immorality of contraception: "There is an inseparable connection, willed by God and unable to be broken by man on his own initiative, between the two meanings of the conjugal act: the unitive meaning and the procreative meaning." The unitive meaning of the conjugal act is that which expresses and strengthens the couple in their love. The procreative meaning is "openness to new life," the continuation of the human race. In artificial insemination, even in marriage, these two meanings of the conjugal act are definitely separated.

Second, the child should be not "the product of medical or biological techniques but the fruit of the conjugal act specific to the love between spouses."

Third, "*in vitro* fertilization is the result of technical action" and "such fertilization is neither in fact achieved nor positively willed as the expression and fruit of a specific of the conjugal union."

Throughout the *Instruction*, Phil, and particularly in the second and third points mentioned, you see a strong contrast between the "technological" and the "personal." The Church raises the question: Just because certain medical or biological techniques are possible, are they by that very fact morally right? The Church obviously believes that technology must be governed by ethics, not the other way around.

I would like to add one last point, Phil. I have found that some people think that the *Instruction* somehow casts a shadow on adoption. This is certainly not intended. The Church has frequently praised the adoptive-parent role as an extraordinary example of Christian love. After all, parents who share their lives with a child in need have an opportunity to love in the same unselfish and unconditional way that Christ loves all his creatures.

19. Is There a Difference Between Active and Passive Euthanasia?

Dear Father,

I am a nurse; I work in the emergency room of a large hospital. The other day I heard a highly placed administrator of the hospital referring to "active" euthanasia and "passive" euthanasia. I have no idea what these terms mean. Can you help me?

Ellie

Dear Ellie,

I'm glad you wrote. One of the unfortunate problems faced by people of today is that the term *euthanasia* is tossed around freely and used in several different senses. So, Ellie, it is important for your moral judgment, for the proper formation of your conscience, to know its precise meaning. In my response to your letter, I would like first to give you an explanation of Catholic moral teaching on euthanasia and then consider a procedure that is not euthanasia at all but is sometimes called "passive euthanasia."

In the Catholic tradition, euthanasia is defined as "an action or omission which of itself or by intention causes death, in order that all suffering may in this way be eliminated" (Congregation for the Doctrine of the Faith, *Declaration on Euthanasia,* 1980). *Active euthanasia* means that the cause of the death is induced, for example, by injecting poison into the body. *Passive euthanasia* means that the cause of death is present within a person but is not resisted when there is a moral obligation to do so. For example, a father of four children refuses a respirator which would help him through an asthma attack, dying because he refused ordinary medical care that was readily available.

From a *moral* point of view, there is no difference between active and passive euthanasia. "Very often," writes Kevin O'Rourke, an expert in healthcare ethics, "people state that active euthanasia is forbidden, but passive euthanasia is acceptable. In the Catholic tradition, there is no significant moral distinction between active and passive euthanasia. Both bespeak causing the death of a sick person when there is a moral obligation to prolong the life of that person" ("Linacre Quarterly," August 1990, page 40).

Since God alone is the Lord of life, and since human beings do not have absolute mastery over life, euthanasia is a grave moral evil. "It is necessary to state firmly once more that nothing and no one can in any way permit the killing of an innocent human being, whether a fetus or an embryo, an infant or an adult, an old person...or a person who is dying" (*Declaration on Euthanasia,* 1980). Euthanasia is morally wrong because it is a violation of God's law ("You shall not kill"), a crime against life, an attack on human dignity in its deepest meaning. Those who practice euthanasia commit the original sin: They take into their own hands the power of God.

Sometimes healthcare professionals, and even moral theologians, use the term *passive euthanasia* to describe the process of allowing a person to die by not continuing extraordinary or disproportionate means of prolonging that person's life. (Perhaps the administrator you refer to in your letter was using "passive euthanasia" in this way.) In truth, the term *euthanasia* should not be used in this case at all. There is an extremely important distinction, Ellie, between "the direct killing of the innocent who are suffering" and "respecting the natural-dying process." From a moral viewpoint, there is all the difference in the world! Direct killing of an innocent human being is gravely wrong, but it does not follow that there is a moral obligation to prolong life by every available means. There are times when "allowing a person to die" is an authentic Christian way of acting.

As you know from your hospital experience, many complex questions arise in which there is tension between the use of medical techniques and the application of moral norms. It may be helpful, therefore, to examine the following question: What guiding moral principles must be used in making these distinctions?

First, it is permissible for a person to choose to use the most modern medical techniques, even if they are experimental.

Second, it is permissible to interrupt these means when the results fall short of expectations or when these means impose on the patient suffering out of proportion to the benefits that he or she may gain by such techniques.

Third, it is always permissible to make-do with the normal means that medicine offers. One is not morally obliged to use techniques that carry heavy burdens with them, such as excessive pain or excessive expense.

Finally, when death is imminent in spite of the means used, it is permissible to refuse forms of treatment that would only secure a prolongation of life, so long as the normal care due to the sick person is not interrupted.

I hope, Ellie, that this response to your letter is helpful to you. It may be that it raises other questions in your mind. If so, let me hear from you again.

---

20. What Is a Living Will?

Dear Father,

At the place where I work, the employees are encouraged to make a living will. I have a few questions: What exactly is a living will? May a Catholic sign such a document? Do you think a living will is really important for a man in his late forties?

Zachary

Dear Zachary,

Your questions are very important. I will give a brief response to each of them in order.

First, what is a living will? It is a formal document — signed, dated, and witnessed by competent persons — in which a person states in advance his or her wishes regarding the use of medical treatments or life-sustaining procedures that might unduly prolong his or her dying process. A copy of this document is then given to one's physician, to one's spouse, and to other appropriate family members — and indeed to anyone who might be involved in critical medical decisions when one is personally unable to express these decisions for oneself.

The growing interest in living wills is especially related, I believe, to a Supreme Court decision of June 25, 1990, in which it was affirmed that states have the right to keep a person alive, unless that person's wishes to the contrary have been clearly spelled out. "The state is justified in requiring that only the patient — expressing oneself clearly and competently — can decide to withdraw treatment." This document is a practical means by which the patient can express himself or herself clearly and competently.

A living will is of tremendous help to a spouse or other family member when a loved one is terminally ill or in a chronic comatose state. Without such an instrument, the next of kin are left helpless either because they do not know their loved one's wishes or because they have no explicit declaration of them. Such a document is an act of kindness to the next of kin because it removes much of the anxiety and fear connected with critical healthcare decisions.

Second, may a Catholic sign a living will? Certainly. At this writing, about forty of the fifty states have a living-will statute. I am not familiar with all of them, but the ones I have seen contain nothing opposed to Catholic teaching. For example, the declaration to be signed and witnessed in the state of Missouri reads as follows: "I have the primary right to make my own decisions concerning treatment that might unduly prolong the dying process. By this declaration I express to my physician, family, and friends my intent. If I should have a terminal condition, it is my desire that my dying not be prolonged by administration of life-prolonging procedures. If my condition is terminal and I am unable to participate in decisions regarding my medical treatment, I direct my attending physician to withhold or withdraw medical procedures that merely prolong the dying process and are not necessary to my comfort or to alleviate pain. It is not my intent to authorize affirmative or deliberate acts or omissions to shorten my life, rather only to permit the natural process of dying."

It seems to me that this declaration clearly rules out euthanasia and is in accord with Catholic teaching on the unnecessary prolongation of the dying process. But if a person were concerned about some aspect of a state statute, that person may formulate his or her own statement. For, as law professor Sandra Johnson has pointed out, "in most states with living-will statutes, an individual is not required to use a particular form in order to execute a legally enforceable living will" (*New Catholic World,* July/August 1987, page 177).

One form that appeals to many people, precisely because of the religious context in which it is framed, is *The Christian Affirmation of Life,* distributed by the Catholic Health Association, 4455 Woodson Road, St. Louis, MO 63134. This affirmation begins with these words of faith: "Because of my Christian belief in the dignity of the human person and my eternal destiny in God, I ask that if I become terminally ill, I be fully informed of the fact so that I can prepare myself emotionally and spiritually to die." It then continues with concrete statements about healthcare.

Third, is it important for a man in his late forties to prepare a living will? I would say "yes." After all, a serious illness or incapacitating accident can happen at any age. The living will is not difficult to formulate; it does not require a great deal of time or effort; and it is of great value to one's next of kin. So why not do it?

I hope, Zachary, that these brief responses to your questions are clear enough. If you or any other reader desires a copy of your state's living-will statute, please request it from the appropriate authority in your state.

---

21. What Is a "Christian Response" to AIDS?

Dear Father,

In one of his recent homilies, our pastor spoke about how we could make the world a better place in which to live. One of the examples he gave was "Make a Christian response to the AIDS crisis." He didn't say anymore about it, but for weeks I've been wondering what is a "Christian response" to AIDS?

Chuck

Dear Chuck,

It goes without saying that I do not know what your pastor had in mind. I must also confess that I am not an expert on AIDS. However, I've read and thought a lot about it, and so I will try to give a response to your question.

AIDS (acquired immune deficiency syndrome) is a relatively new and as yet medically incurable pathological condition. Though its full effects have not yet been felt, many experts consider that it is already an epidemic in the United States.

This epidemic, and the human suffering related to it, raises many complex moral questions: for example, about testing, about confidentiality, about the delivery of healthcare. I could not attempt to treat such questions in a short space, even if the answers were clear. And they are definitely not clear at this time.

In an effort to answer your letter, however, I think you might profit from examining three other questions:

1. Is AIDS a direct punishment from God?
2. What moral lessons can be learned from the AIDS crisis?
3. What can be done to help people with AIDS?

Concerning the first question, some religious preachers, especially on radio and television, are confidently stating that God is the direct agent of AIDS, that the epidemic is a divine retribution against homosexuals and drug users.

This kind of preaching seems to me to be not only gratuitous but also unchristian. It certainly attempts to "read the mind of God." If God directly punishes sinners with physical illness, then why doesn't he punish the murderers, rapists, and terrorists in the same way? Does anyone actually believe that God uses such a selective process for punishment?

More importantly, Chuck, this approach certainly portrays a strange image of God, especially as God is revealed in the New Testament. Jesus, for example, is not seen vindictively throwing stones at the adulterous woman, striking down the woman at Jacob's well, tossing the tax collector out of the Temple, making sure that the hardhearted chief priests and elders were afflicted by an incurable disease.

I believe that Cardinal Bernardin of Chicago is much closer to the Christian mark when he says that "God is loving and compassionate, not vengeful. Made in God's image, every human being is of inestimable worth....The gospel reveals that while Jesus did not hesitate to proclaim a radical ethic of life...he never ceased to reach out to the lowly, to the outcasts of his time, even if they did not live up to the full demands of his teaching." This echoes what Pope John Paul II said to AIDS patients in San Francisco in 1987: "God loves us without distinction, without limit. He loves those of you who are sick, those who are suffering from AIDS and from AIDS-related complex" (*The Many Faces of AIDS: A Gospel Response,* #71).

William Spohn, S.J., has insightfully pointed out the dire consequences of seeing AIDS as a direct punishment from God. In this case, "the Almighty can be conveniently enlisted to justify righteous rejection and discrimination. If the plague can be attributed to God, believers can leave the victims in their well-merited suffering....It also undermines any compassionate response of the churches to the enormous suffering caused by this epidemic" (*Theological Studies,* March 1988, page 106).

Obviously, Chuck, AIDS is *not* a direct punishment from God.

Concerning the second question, it may be that the AIDS epidemic can urge people to see again the value of their Christian/Catholic moral teaching. Much of this teaching is based on the natural law. This is an inner law that rational men and women can grasp because, as Saint Paul says, it is "written in their hearts" (Romans 2:15). They can come to at least basic principles of morality by reflecting upon their own natures, drives, and relationships.

Catholic sexual morality, which is often casually dismissed these days, insists that human conduct needs to observe certain natural purposes and accept certain natural limitations. Thus, sexual promiscuity and certain sexual practices are "against nature," as created by God, and are not protected from serious consequences. Truly, "You can't fool Mother Nature."

The modern experience of AIDS seems to reinforce the wisdom of Catholic teaching that sexual intercourse finds its rightful place only in marriage, with one's lifelong partner. Similarly, intravenous drug usage for purposes of a "high," and without medical supervision, is a risk-filled practice against which human nature often rebels.

What I am saying here, Chuck, is that a Christian response to

AIDS should make people reevaluate their moral behavior. It still surprises me that so many experts, in an admirable effort to control the spread of AIDS, recommend "safe sex" and "clean needles" rather than strongly challenging persons to change their behavior. In this case, as in so many others, perhaps the old saying is true: God helps those who help themselves. People can help themselves by listening to the voice of reason and the tradition of Christian morality.

Concerning the third question, it is clear that the AIDS epidemic offers a tremendous challenge to everyone's charity and ministry. Since curing people with AIDS is at present not possible, caring for them is the only option. Experts suggest that AIDS patients are best cared for in hospices rather than in hospitals. These hospices will certainly be multiplying in the years ahead and will need professional healthcare workers as well as many volunteers to staff them. Who will be the volunteers?

Understandably, Chuck, many people are reluctant to care for (or even come close to) AIDS patients. This is due in part to the vast amount of misinformation that still surrounds this issue; but it is also due to people's self-protecting fear. What can be done about this fear? The Canadian Catholic Bishops answered that question recently when they wrote, "We must do all we can to overcome it because there is danger that fear will sap the energies we need to face this disease." AIDS is not just a "gay disease" or a "druggie's disease." It is, after all, a human disease. For a long time to come, it will challenge the Christian compassion of the entire world.

22. How Can I Deal With My Anger?

Dear Father,
    I am in my mid forties and am struggling more than ever with angry feelings. I feel guilty after I lose my temper, but

I'm not sure what I'm doing wrong or what I should be doing. I am open to suggestions.

Ray

Dear Ray,

I know that it is an oversimplification but perhaps not too far off the mark to say that people deal with anger in one of three basic ways.

There are certain persons who regularly give full vent to their anger by "flying off the handle" with moans and groans and much cursing and swearing. Such behavior resembles that of spoiled children who have not yet learned how to deal with their emotions; it is certainly not appropriate for mature adults.

I have noticed over the years that persons who handle anger in this way are usually shunned by others, when possible, and tend to be lonely and isolated individuals. Moreover, when such behavior is chronic, it may well be a sign of deep emotional disturbance. Professional counseling may be called for.

There is also a large number of people, however, who deal with anger in a quite different way. They suppress it, refuse to acknowledge it, pretend that it isn't there. They stuff their angry feelings into their psyche and hope these feelings will go away. But, of course, they don't go away. They keep roaming around looking for other ways to rear their ugly heads. They contribute to brooding, to restlessness, to resentment, even to real depression.

Between these two extremes — giving violent vent to anger on the one hand and suppressing it on the other — there is, I believe, a constructive and Christian way to deal with angry feelings. Let me offer you an outline of this approach.

First, you should allow yourself to acknowledge your angry feelings and take a good look at them. Angry feelings in and of themselves are not sinful; they are, in fact, unavoidable. But you can learn from them. Where are they coming from? Why does this or that imagined or real slight arouse such strong feelings in you? What is the underlying cause of your anger?

Second, you should allow yourself to talk about your angry feelings when this is reasonably possible. It is extremely helpful when family members or coworkers or neighbors can sit down and talk about the anger that has flared in their relationships. In family relationships, particularly, it is important to develop the habit of talking about angry feelings even over rather small and insignificant issues. Then when big issues do arise, the positive pattern will be set.

Third, you should try to contain your anger and not let it overflow its boundaries. If you do not exercise control, you may find that disagreement with a small decision at work can fester into hatred of the whole company, even the entire free-enterprise system. A snide remark by a priest, for example, can lead to resentment against the bishop, the pope, and even God himself!

Fourth, you should try to develop the virtue that takes the wind out of anger: namely, the virtue of humility. As I mentioned, you can learn from your anger. I believe that anger tells you something about yourself: You may have made your opinions and ideas and ways of doing things superimportant. You may have made yourself a "know-it-all" and resent any slight against your self-made importance.

Humility teaches you that you can relax, that you don't have to put on airs, that you can be yourself. It reminds you that God loves and accepts you as you are. It trains you to laugh at yourself rather than to take yourself so seriously that you are forever angry at something.

I hope, Ray, that these suggestions are helpful to you in dealing with your angry feelings.

23. What Can I Do About Jealousy?

Dear Father,

I've been going with a wonderful girl for about a year. I'm hoping that some day we will get married. She says I'm too jealous of her and this bugs her. She is probably right. But I don't understand jealousy or where it comes from or what to do about it.

Steve

Dear Steve,

You are not alone in your problems with jealousy. For most people, I believe, jealousy is easy to experience but hard to define. One way to get a handle on jealousy is to compare it to envy. Sometimes the words *envy* and *jealousy* are used interchangeably; but they are quite different.

Jealousy has to do with persons; envy, with things. Jealousy is a fear of losing another's special love; envy is resentment at or a desire to possess what another has. Jealousy is dread of being replaced by a rival; envy is a kind of sadness over the good fortune of another. For example, Steve, you are jealous of your girlfriend because you are afraid someone may steal her away from you. If you were envious of your neighbor's Jaguar or his salary increase, it would be because his having more than you seems to make you less of a person.

The poet John Dryden once called jealousy "the jaundice of the soul." He was right. Jealousy is a kind of spiritual sickness that turns trust to suspicion and love to hate. It is also a spreading sickness. It infects the jealous person, of course, but also the person who is the object of jealousy. It may affect a good many other people as well.

Where does jealousy come from? It comes from immaturity. The jealous person is marked by a preoccupation with self. Intense, unreasoning, self-centered jealousy is a sure sign of immaturity. An old saying expresses it this way: "In jealousy there is more self-love than true love." Or, in the words of Saint Paul, "Love is not jealous."

I believe a lot of people are fooled by jealousy. They may think "a little bit" of jealousy is charming. But it is one of the most destructive of human emotions. Sooner or later the green-eyed monster gobbles up all true love. Jealousy feeds on suspicion, erodes trust, arouses hostility. In the vivid image of Hubert Van Zeller, "Jealousy finds a rosebush and leaves a stick."

What can be done about jealousy? Unfortunately, Steve, there is no magic potion that will cure it. The jealous person must start by being ruthlessly honest with himself or herself. As I said above, people can be fooled by jealousy, pretending it is "cute." But it must be seen for what it is: a deadly poison that destroys love and friendship. The jealous person must drop the hundred and one excuses that "justify" his or her jealousy. It must be seen as a deliberating disease. It needs surgery, not excuses.

The jealous person must begin to deal with his or her immaturity as a person and as a Christian. In other words, the jealous person must begin to grow up! Consider the following contrasts:

- The jealous person demands the center of the stage at all times, must at every moment be "the one and only." The mature Christian, on the other hand, is humble, open, not graspingly possessive.
- The jealous person is forever suspicious and judgmental. The mature Christian is trusting and tolerant.
- The jealous person mistakenly believes that he or she can demand affection and love. The mature person knows that love and affection are gifts one can only receive with gratitude.
- The jealous person childishly thinks that he or she can push open the door of another's heart and demand entrance into another's life. The mature Christian knows that love must be built slowly and carefully and that in the house of love there

will always be "secret rooms" where even the friend or lover cannot go.

The sickness of jealousy can be cured, Steve, but only if you will take the hard medicine to cure it. Good luck!

---

24. How Much Should I Give to the Poor?

Dear Father,
Every time I receive a request in the mail seeking money for the poor, I feel that I must send a donation because God may have caused this request to come to me. I really believe in helping the poor, but I am getting loads of mail from many organizations. I try to send a small donation to each, but it is a losing game. If I selected a certain number of them and concentrated on them, do you think God would be pleased or not? The gospel about "the sheep and the goats" is a frightening thing.

Frank

Dear Frank,

I would like to thank you for raising a good question. Many good people have struggled with the same problem. It deserves serious attention.

I would also like to express my admiration for your truly Christian attitude toward the poor and needy. The gospel about the sheep and goats (see Matthew 25:31-46) is certainly central to the teaching of Jesus. It is all too easy for Christians to forget that Jesus makes charity the criterion for Final Judgment. Responding or not responding to the needs of the hungry and homeless and the ill and imprisoned becomes the final issue.

In response to your letter, Frank, here are several guidelines that highlight the virtue of Christian charity on the one hand and the virtue of Christian prudence on the other.

The first point to be stressed is that there is no moral obligation to respond to all the requests you receive through the mail. I do not mean to imply that these requests are unworthy of consideration; it's just that there are so many of them. Direct-mail campaigns have multiplied in recent years. They are becoming more and more sophisticated. There is no end in sight. While it is certainly true that all people have a moral obligation to help the poor, it is equally true that they cannot do everything. They have to draw practical and realistic lines somewhere.

There is a general principle of Christian morality that can help you in drawing these lines. Venerable and practical, it is called "the principle of well-ordered charity." According to this principle, your financial resources should be used to help care for the needs of your family...then the needs of your local neighborhood and parish...then those of the larger community and Church. Moreover, this well-ordered charity can be done only according to your means. YOU cannot give what you haven't got. If you follow this principle in an honest way, you will find that it is very helpful in making decisions of conscience.

When you receive "premiums" that come through the mail with requests for donations, don't worry about keeping them even though you have not sent a contribution. You are not morally obliged to return the calendars, gummed labels, statues that glow in the dark, or other such items. The sender assumes the risk in sending them. Even if you do not make a donation as requested, there is no injustice in using these things.

The second point to be emphasized is that there is no reason why you should feel guilty or fearful because you cannot respond to all appeals. Like everyone else, you have to accept your limitations, financial and otherwise. You cannot take all the problems of the world on your own shoulders and lose your peace and joy because you are unable to solve all of them. Certainly, "the Lord loves a cheerful giver," but the Lord also understands your limitations.

As with many other things involving money, so too with giving to charity: A planned approach is usually helpful. I suggest that you try to determine what you are able to give to charity, choose a few charities that seem especially worthy, help these according to your ability, and leave the rest in the hands of God. This approach will help you fulfill the law of the gospel and at the same time give you peace of mind.

25. Is Racism a Sin?

Dear Father,

For twenty-five years I have been involved in works of social justice. I must say I am disappointed with the Catholic Church for not condemning racism. After all, racism is a sin, isn't it?

Larry

Dear Larry,

I do not know how to answer your letter. I doubt that I can ease your disappointment with the Church, but your letter raises several questions that should be answered.

First, what is meant by racism? Racism is a conviction based on a theory that some human beings are inherently superior and others essentially inferior precisely because of race. Racism expresses itself through racial discrimination: that is, the unjust or unequal treatment of individual persons, not because of their faults or failings or their lack of ability or merit but simply because they are members of a certain race.

Second, is racism a sin? It certainly is. Racism denies the essential unity of the human race. It is an insult to the dignity of certain people whom God has made in his image and likeness. It is a violation of both justice and charity.

Third, is it true to say that the Catholic Church has not condemned racism? Quite the contrary! The Church is strongly on record as condemning this moral evil. The Second Vatican Council said that racial discrimination "is incompatible with God's design" and emphasized that "the Church reproves, as foreign to the mind of Christ, any discrimination against people or any harassment of them on the basis of their race, color, condition in life, or religion" (*Declaration on the Relationships of the Church to Non-Christian Religions,* #5).

For eleven years Pope John Paul II, the chief pastor of the Catholic Church, has repeatedly condemned racism. In March 1988, for example, he called racial discrimination "a painful wound that still exists in various parts of the world" and admonished Christian people to "avoid any behavior favoring or maintaining any form of racial discrimination."

Closer to home, the United States Catholic Bishops have frequently condemned racism. In their moving pastoral letter, *Brothers and Sisters to Us,* the bishops wrote: "Racism is a sin: a sin that divides the human family, blots out the image of God among specific members of that family, and violates the fundamental human dignity of those called to be children of the same Father. Racism is the sin that says some human beings are inherently superior and others essentially inferior because of race. It is the sin that makes racial characteristics the determining factor for the exercise of human rights" (#9).

Even these few samples of Catholic teaching (and they could easily be multiplied) show that the Church does indeed condemn racism, pronouncing it a sin. That is not to say, however, that the Church has done enough. The Church must continue to oppose racism wherever it appears, in its own institutions as well as those of secular society. The Church must also continue to try to convince Catholics that racism is not an option but a sin. Certainly, there are still many Catholics — clergy and laity alike — who seem to take racism for granted. One wonders if they would ever include racial discrimination in their examination of conscience or ever confess it as a sin.

At the same time there are many Catholics who join hands with other Americans to promote programs that have been successful in rooting out racial discrimination from today's society. Together, they are committed to racial justice in housing, education, healthcare, and employment. The future of the American dream may well depend on the efforts of such people. For, as the United States Catholic Bishops put it, "There must be no turning back along the road of justice, no sighing for bygone times of privilege, no nostalgia for simple solutions from another age. For we are children of the age to come, when the first shall be last and the last first, when blessed are they who serve Christ the Lord in all His brothers and sisters, especially those who are poor and suffer injustice" (*Brothers and Sisters to Us*, #59).

I congratulate you, Larry, on your work for social justice, and remind you that the Church is on your side.

26. Is There a Handy Moral Code for Employees?

Dear Father,

A few evenings ago I was involved in a long and interesting discussion about many areas of right and wrong. The discussion settled on what I would call the duties of employees toward employers. I've been wondering if there is a handy moral code somewhere about these matters?

Kevin

Dear Kevin,

I am not sure if there is a "handy moral code" about the duties of employees, but perhaps I could help you by stating three basic principles of justice that apply to employees and some examples that may make them more practical.

The first principle is this: Employees are bound in justice to work conscientiously and fairly in return for their wages. This statement embraces the employee's side of the work contract. The employee agrees, either formally or informally, to do a day's work for a day's pay; but agreement is frequently compromised in the workplace. Often — in many different ways — this principle is violated by

- Workers who loaf away hour after hour in idle conversation with fellow workers or on the telephone with family or friends.
- Workers who use much of their on-the-job time in taking care of personal or family business, for example, paying bills, computing their taxes, and the like.
- Workers who extend the lunch period or coffee break to unreasonable limits.

Employees who do such things would probably agree that they do them only when it's fairly certain they won't get caught. In other words, they know that these practices are not honest, but they slide into them anyway. They are, in fact, violations of justice.

The second principle is this: Employees are bound in justice to respect the property rights of their employers. Think of the many ways in which this principle is transgressed by

- Workers who take for their own use and benefit goods and materials that rightly belong to their employers. This pilfering may range from small supplies, such as pencils and paper clips, to expensive materials, such as steel, lumber, electrical equipment, or medicine. A man who was taking one of my classes in Christian ethics once described this practice as "one of

America's favorite indoor sports." It is certainly not uncommon. Yet it is really a form of stealing.

- Workers who neglect to take reasonable care of the equipment and material they make use of in the performance of their jobs. People who would handle a home computer with kid gloves may treat a company computer like a pile of junk. And so it is with other equipment "that doesn't belong to me."
- Workers who in one way or another pad their expense accounts, demanding recompense from their employers for expenses not actually incurred. A modern American trick is to disguise immoral activities in veiled language, for example, "I misspoke" instead of "I lied." So, too, "I padded my expense account" sounds better than "I lied and cheated and stole."

The third principle is this: Employees are bound in justice to respect the good name and reputation of their employers. More often than you may think, Kevin, this obligation is ignored by

- Workers who have gained knowledge of their employer's past failures or secret sins and spread this knowledge far and wide. (In Catholic moral theology, this is called detraction.)
- Workers who tell lies about their employers in order to justify themselves or who exaggerate small faults into monstrous crimes. (This is called slander.)

It may seem to some people that these principles and examples are almost too basic. There is a lot of talk these days about how "complex" things are and "there are not many white-or-black areas but a lot of gray ones." To be sure, there are complicated moral situations in the workaday world, but I think these basic principles of justice still apply and do provide a "handy moral code" for most employees.

I once received a small homemade plaque from a friend who shared my admiration for one of our great popes, Pope Leo XIII.

A hundred years ago Pope Leo wrote about the moral obligation of employees. These are the words on the plaque:

Duties of Employees

To perform entirely and conscientiously
Whatever work has been freely and
equitably agreed upon;
Not in any way to injure the property
Or harm the person of my employer.

Now that I think of it, Kevin, this may be the handy moral code you were looking for.

27. Is There a Handy Moral Code for Employers?

Dear Father,
I was angered when I read (in our church bulletin) your answer to Kevin in which you gave a handy moral code for employees. What about the other side? You laid it on the line for employees, so now lay it on the line for employers. Isn't there a handy moral code for them too?

Bill

Dear Bill,

I am sorry that my answer to Kevin angered you. It would have been helpful to me if you told me what particular items made you upset. In my answer to Kevin, I certainly did not mean to imply that only employees have moral obligations. Employers certainly have moral obligations toward their employees.

These obligations arise from the very nature of the relationship between the employer and the employee. The employee has certain basic rights that must always be respected by the employer. Though this matter can become very complicated, I will try to deal with the essentials by stating three principles of social justice that clearly apply to employers, and then I will offer some specific obligations that flow from these principles.

The first principle is this: The employer is morally bound to respect the human dignity of his or her employees. Pope John Paul II, in his 1981 encyclical *On Human Work,* insists that this principle, which he calls "the primacy of persons over things," is one of the most important of all.

Certain concrete requirements flow from this principle: Employers are obliged to provide a work environment that is not harmful to the employees' physical health or moral integrity; they are also obliged not to impose more work than human strength can endure nor "that kind of work which is unsuited to a worker's age or sex" (Pope Leo XIII).

The second principle is this: The employer is bound in conscience to pay the employee a just wage. Pope John Paul II reaffirmed the constant teaching of the Church on this matter: "The key problem of social ethics in this case is that of just remuneration for work done. In the context of the present, there is no more important way of securing a just relationship between the worker and the employer than that constituted by remuneration for work" (*On Human Work,* #19).

To be sure, many complex questions arise about this moral obligation. They cannot all be treated here. There are, however, certain generalizations that flow from the social teaching of the Church:

(a) The minimum just wage should be determined by the very reason why a person works, namely, to earn a livelihood. It seems to me that whenever the minimum wage is debated in today's society, heavy emphasis is placed on how the increase of the minimum wage will affect the employer. Very little seems to be said about the basic needs of the employee.

(b) The just wage must take into consideration the requirements of the family. In the words of John Paul II: "Just remuneration for the work of an adult who is responsible for a family means remuneration which will suffice for establishing and properly maintaining a family and providing security for its future" (*On Human Work*, #19). I am aware that for a number of reasons this idea of a family living wage has never been widely accepted in America. Perhaps this is one reason for the sad decline of the American family.

(c) Women employees have a right to receive equal wages for equal work. It is quite remarkable that after decades of the women's movement and after countless efforts to raise consciousness concerning discrimination against women in the workplace, wage discrimination still flourishes. The fact that it still flourishes does not make it right; it is just a reminder of how hard it is to root out social injustice.

The third principle is this: The employer has a moral obligation to provide basic social benefits intended to ensure the life and health of employees and their families. Pope John Paul II emphasizes the basic benefits of health insurance, rest, and retirement pensions. This is what he says: "The expenses involved in health care, especially in the case of accidents at work, demand that medical assistance should be easily available for workers and that as far as possible it should be cheap or even free of charge. Another sector regarding benefits is the sector associated with the right to rest. In the first place this involves a regular weekly rest comprising at least Sunday and also a longer period of rest, namely the holiday or vacation....A third sector concerns the right to a pension and to insurance for old age and in case of accidents at work" (*On Human Work*, #19).

I think you would agree with me, Bill, that today's society generally acknowledges these moral responsibilities of employers. Many of them, sometimes only after brutal labor-management battles, have been enacted into law or are demanded by government regulation. Certainly, there are many employers who sincerely strive to put these principles into practice in their workaday world. There are some who do not, and their sin "cries to heaven for vengeance." History reveals that the relationship between employer and employee will be governed either by the moral law or the law of the jungle. It is wise for us to remember that the law of the jungle is never completely tamed.

28. What Does the Church Say About Interfaith Marriages?

Dear Father,

David, my nephew and godson, is getting serious about marriage. He's Catholic, his fiancée is Protestant. He often asks me for information and has already raised a few questions about interfaith marriages. For example, could he be allowed to get married in her church? In general, what does the Catholic Church say about interfaith marriages?

Aunt Margaret

Dear Aunt Margaret,

At the risk of being misunderstood and causing hard feelings, I think it is fair to say that the Catholic Church, like most religions, does not really favor interfaith marriages. I know that this position strikes some people as narrow prejudice, but in truth it is based on long experience with the special difficulties of such marriages.

What are some of these difficulties? Religion should be a bond of unity in marriage; in interfaith marriages it can easily become a bone of contention. This is especially true when children come upon the scene. Common worship by parents and children is almost impossible. The religious education of the children also raises tough questions. I have found over the years that young couples tend to dismiss these problems before marriage but then struggle with them after marriage.

This is not to say that interfaith marriages can never be successful. Some are remarkably so. Yet their success demands a realistic understanding of the problems that may be met along the way and an extraordinary generosity in dealing with these problems. Some couples enter such an interfaith marriage without considering the potential problems and then find they are not capable of great generosity, at least not over the long haul. Thus, religious issues become marriage and family issues as well.

While not favoring interfaith marriages, the Catholic Church certainly wants to offer pastoral support to those couples who enter such marriages. This support emphasizes how important it is for the couple to prepare themselves as well as possible for such marriages. Both the Catholic party and the non-Catholic party should be aware of mutual expectations and potential hazards. In addition to the preparation that applies to all marriages, there are certain points that apply precisely to interfaith marriages. I would like to touch on these points here, but with the caution that dioceses and parishes may handle these matters in somewhat different ways. Concrete information on procedures and requirements can be obtained from any Catholic parish.

First, because the Catholic faith has many implications for marriage and family life, the non-Catholic party is asked to spend some time learning about basic Catholic beliefs and practices. The purpose of this is not to try to convert the non-Catholic but to inform him or her of the religious values and obligations of the Catholic party. It is equally important, I believe, that the Catholic party become familiar with the religious beliefs and practices of his or her future spouse.

Second, the Catholic who wishes to marry a non-Catholic needs the express permission of the bishop of the diocese (Canon 1124). This permission is usually requested through one's parish priest. The bishop will grant it if there is a good reason and provided the norms of the Church are fulfilled.

Third, the Catholic party in an interfaith marriage has to make a declaration "that he or she is prepared to remove dangers of falling away from the faith" and must make "a sincere promise to do all in his or her power to have all the children baptized and brought up in the Catholic Church" (Canon 1125, #1). I know from experience that this can be a very touchy issue. It is essential, therefore, that the non-Catholic party have a clear understanding of this declaration and promise. Very early in the preparation of an interfaith marriage, it seems to me, the couple should discuss this matter most carefully.

Fourth, Catholics are obliged to be married in the presence of an authorized priest or deacon and two witnesses. In interfaith marriages the pastor of the non-Catholic party is usually invited to take part in the ceremony. For the Catholic party to be married before a non-Catholic minister in a non-Catholic church, the express permission of the bishop is required (Canon 1127, #2). This is usually requested through one's parish priest. If it is granted, a Catholic priest or deacon may be present and take some part in the ceremony, but this is not absolutely required.

I hope this reply is helpful to you and to others who may be looking for the same information. The information, as I have outlined it here, may seem rather cold and legalistic. But it is the hope of the Church that solid preparation will help a couple avoid some of the potential drawbacks of an interfaith marriage and live their marriage in a positive and happy way.